Peak Performance

Published by Accent Press Ltd – 2013

ISBN 9781908917553

The Quick Reads project in Wales is an initiative coordinated by the Welsh Books Council and supported by the Welsh Government.

Printed and bound by CPI Group (UK) Ltd, Croydon, CR0 4YY

Cover design by Madamadari
Cover photo by Benjamin Stephens

CYNGOR LLYFRAU CYMRU
WELSH BOOKS COUNCIL

Noddir gan
Lywodraeth Cymru
Sponsored by
Welsh Government

Peak Performance

Tori James

ACCENT PRESS LTD

To my family, friends and colleagues – thank you for your never-ending support and encouragement. You are the inspiration in my life and the people who give me the energy and enthusiasm to take on new challenges.

To my young cousins Mark, Eve, Rebecca, Eleanor, Huw, Evan and Tom – I hope that you will all embark on some exciting adventures of your own one day, and treasure the beautiful countryside we have in Wales and the UK.

Introduction

Mount Everest is the highest mountain in the world. Standing at 8,850 metres high, its black, wind-ravaged peak dominates the Himalayan mountain range.

For hundreds of years this natural wonder has both terrified and fascinated climbers and explorers. In 1953 Sir Edmund Hillary and Tenzing Norgay made history when they risked their lives to become the first people to reach the rooftop of the world.

Today, Everest remains one of the most dangerous places on earth. Every year hundreds of climbers try to reach the summit and many do not return home. Their bodies lie where they have fallen, in icy graves on the mountain.

The dangers are clear. Temperatures are below –20°C, the air is thin and there is the constant threat of avalanches and rockfalls. But the achievement of reaching the top of the world is so great that people are willing to risk everything to get there.

For some, climbing Everest is a childhood dream but for me it was all about the challenge of doing something I never thought was possible.

Becoming the first Welsh woman and the youngest British female to reach the summit of Everest in 2007 was the proudest moment of my life. The lessons I've learnt along the way are not from physically reaching the top, but from the journey, both on and off the mountain. I believe the secret of success is being passionate about the things you do in your life; it's about thorough planning and never giving up even when the going gets tough.

Everyone has their own personal goals and dreams. I hope this book will show that if a 5' 1" farm girl from Pembrokeshire can succeed in climbing the world's highest mountain, you too can achieve your dreams. All you need is self-belief and a can-do attitude.

Chapter One

THE YOUNG EXPLORER

I'm sure that my taste for adventure started before I was born. On 10 December 1981, the snow was falling heavily on my family's farm in Pembrokeshire. My mum and dad watched as the giant flakes hid their car and covered the tracks. And that's when I decided it was time to make my entrance into the world.

As Mum went into labour, Dad went to dig out his old Land Rover and they made the slow and slippery nine-mile journey from our home to Withybush Hospital in Haverfordwest, where four hours later, at 4 p.m., I was born – exactly on time.

I like to think that being born in a blizzard is the reason why I love cold, wintry, snow-covered places. I grew up on a dairy farm with my younger sister, Olivia, so being outdoors in all weather was natural to us. My dad, Richard, was born on the family farm and has lived there all his life, just like his father and grandfather before him. He met my mum, Jane, at a Young Farmers' dance when she was a teenager.

Living on a farm, surrounded by dangerous machinery and animals, I learnt to respect the power of nature and understand the risks. We kept a herd of more than a hundred milking cows and sixty beef cattle, which needed constant attention. I have vivid memories of my parents coming into the kitchen on many occasions, soaking wet and covered in cow muck, after being out in the fields looking after the animals. Being farmers, there was never a chance of putting off a task until the rain stopped. It was an all-weather way of life.

I would often help out feeding the calves. And seeing Mum and Dad working equally hard on the farm, there was never any question that women were not as strong or capable as men.

I was four years old when my nan gave me an important piece of advice, which I have carried with me throughout my life. I was helping her to bake a Victoria sponge in her kitchen. Struggling to get the lid off the jam jar, I turned to her and said, 'I can't do it, Nan. Will you try?' and handed the jar to her. She took it from me, looked at the jam jar, then looked at me and announced, 'There's no such word as can't. Try again,' and passed the jar back to me. I tried again and the second time the top popped off. It was a lesson that has stuck with me throughout my life and helped me whenever I have felt like giving up.

At school, my favourite subject was geography and it still is. Even at primary school I was fascinated by the water cycle and water's power to erode landscapes and carve features into rock. From the age of eleven I attended two boarding schools. Living away from home was daunting at first but then it became an adventure all of its own and I loved every minute of it.

Throughout my teenage years I thrived on being active and was always looking for things to do. I joined the 4th Haverfordwest Girl Guides, where I learned to camp, light and cook on open fires and work as a team. One of my fondest memories is the time we went on a trip to Switzerland. Our leaders chose a small group of girls to go hiking in the early hours of the morning to watch dawn break over the mountains. It was such an adventure, climbing steep, rocky paths in complete darkness, listening to the cow bells in the distance. I felt intrepid, and that same feeling of excitement when venturing into the unknown in the dark still remains with me today when I am out in the mountains.

At fourteen I got the chance to plan and carry out an expedition on my own when I started the Duke of Edinburgh's Award. The Award encourages young people to challenge themselves through a series of different activities, including volunteering, physical challenges and learning new skills. Working with four other girls I completed Bronze and Silver levels and then aimed for the highest level Gold Award. For this my team had to plan a 50-mile route in a remote area of the UK over four days. Carrying our camping equipment on our backs, we walked for miles across mountains and rivers. Our legs were tired, our knees sore and our feet in blisters. But the excitement of reaching the finish and being presented with a Gold Award made it all worthwhile, and left me wanting more.

During my final year at school I joined a youth expedition run by British Exploring. Founded by Surgeon Commander Murray Levick, a member of Scott's Antarctic Expedition of 1912–13, British Exploring is a youth charity steeped in history. It offers young people the chance to take part in adventures and environmental research projects in remote places of the world like the Amazon rainforest or the Arctic. My parents allowed me to apply to join an expedition to the Land of Fire and Ice, learning to ice-climb and abseil on the Vatnajökull glacier in Iceland. Out of hundreds of teenagers who applied I was picked for one of the forty-five places but my parents could not afford to fund it all, so I had to start organising events, including a school concert, disco and pool tournament. It was a busy time, planning my expedition and revising for my A-level exams.

The expedition to Iceland was everything I had dreamed of. For four weeks, I was on the greatest expedition ever. It was the longest time I had ever been away from home. Arriving in Iceland felt like we had landed on the moon. The landscape was barren and rocky; there was no greenery, just grey and black jagged rocks formed by volcanic activity and the white of the glacier. We camped out in sub-zero conditions and I was taught how to use a rope, iceaxe and crampons – spikes strapped onto my walking boots – to grip the ice as I climbed up the glaciers. We spent hours mapping the crevasses on the surface of the glacier. I also learnt about the dangers of snow-covered holes in the ice when I fell waist-deep into a crevasse cutting the under-side of my arms and elbows. My group was led by a team of scientists and mountaineers. Among the leaders was Ben Stephens, a twenty-year-old geography student from Oxford University. Ben had already been on several overseas expeditions and he knew a lot about glaciers and Iceland. Secretly I fancied him. I thought he was fantastic, charismatic and incredibly good-looking, too. His passion for the subject was infectious and I spoke to him about it at every opportunity, borrowing his text books.

The four weeks in this icy wilderness had sparked more than just a spirit of adventure and I knew more expeditions would follow.

Chapter Two

'DO YOU WANT TO CLIMB EVEREST?'

In 2003 I found my first job, working as an office assistant at the charity which had organised my trip to Iceland, British Exploring. For a young adventurer it was an exciting time. I had graduated from Royal Holloway, University of London, with a degree in geography and I was working amongst people whose lives revolved around the outdoors.

My office was based in the Royal Geographical Society headquarters in South Kensington, which is one of the world's leading centres for promoting geography and scientific research. As a student I had visited many times to listen to lectures by the most famous explorers in the world, like Pen Hadow, the first person to trek solo to the North and South Poles, and Italian mountaineer Reinhold Messner, who was the first climber to reach the summit of Everest without oxygen. On several occasions, as I walked to my desk, I found myself sharing a lift with TV environmentalist

David Bellamy or I would pass world-famous explorer Sir Ranulph Fiennes in the corridor.

I also started dating Ben, whom I'd met on that glacier in Iceland. He was two years older than me, and incredibly ambitious, confident and outgoing. We were both passionate about exploring and taking on new personal goals and worked well together. Ben was studying for a Master of Business Administration degree at London Business School, with future plans to run his own business, or perhaps 'take over the world', as his dad joked. Often we talked about travel and expeditions and another challenge.

One day Ben casually said: 'I'm thinking of climbing Mount Everest. Do you want to do it too?'

I looked at him in amazement. 'Don't be so stupid,' I said, dismissing the idea completely.

Everest was huge, more than eight times higher than Wales's tallest mountain, Snowdon. I thought I could never climb the world's highest mountain. 'I'll support and help you all I can,' I replied. 'And maybe I'll come with you as far as Base Camp.' I knew that even that would take an eighteen-day trek.

But Everest kept gnawing at me. Perhaps I was capable of climbing it. I knew I could cope with the extreme endurance and freezing conditions. Just six months earlier I had made the news headlines when I was part of the Pink Lady PoleCats. Together with two of my work friends from British Exploring, we were the first all-female team to complete the Polar Challenge, a 360-mile race across the icy wastelands of northern Canada and the frozen seas of the Arctic Ocean to the magnetic North Pole. We had skied for eighteen days in temperatures of −20°C to finish the race in sixth place out of sixteen teams.

'You do realise that no other Welsh woman has climbed to the summit?' Ben informed me. 'And if we go next year, you'll be the youngest British female to do it, too.'

At the time Scottish climber Polly Murray held the record by reaching the summit of Everest at the age of twenty-six. If we completed our expedition in 2007 I would be twenty-five. With that nugget of information, Ben caught my attention. This was my chance to represent Wales and make history. We spent the rest of the evening, and weeks afterwards, trawling the internet for facts and statistics, learning about all the great climbers in history who had conquered the mountain they called the rooftop of the world.

It seemed that Mount Everest had always held a fascination for explorers. It was even named after a Welshman – Sir George Everest who had, in 1823, led a survey which first mapped out the Himalayas and confirmed Everest as the highest mountain in the world.

I read about the many early attempts in the 1920s and 1930s when explorers risked everything to be the first to conquer the world's highest mountain. I read about the mystery of British explorers George Mallory and Andrew 'Sandy' Irvine who disappeared in the mists of Everest in 1924. Seventy-five years later Mallory's body was found on the North Face and to this day no one knows if they made it to the summit. I read about the expeditions in the 1950s which attempted to open up a new route through Nepal after the Chinese government stopped western climbers passing through Tibet. And I read the front page of *The Times* newspaper on the morning of Queen Elizabeth II's Coronation in 1953 which broke the news that Edmund Hillary and his guide, Sherpa Tenzing Norgay, had earned their place in mountaineering history when they reached the highest point on Earth.

During our research we discovered there were very few women listed among the names of those who had reached the summit. Rebecca Stephens was the first British woman to climb to the summit, in May 1993. There was Alison Hargreaves, the first woman to climb without oxygen; 51-year-old Vicky Jack, the oldest woman; the first American woman was Stacy Allison and the first Irish woman Clare O'Leary. But no mention of a Welsh woman – I started to think that maybe it was time to change that.

I began reading *High Adventure*, Edmund Hillary's account of his 1953 conquest, and was fascinated by his story of triumph over nature's greatest obstacle. I considered Everest way beyond my reach, but was it? After the Polar Challenge, achieving the seemingly impossible was starting to become an addiction. I wanted again to experience that inner pride and elation that came with success. It was also an opportunity to make history and I couldn't let it pass. I knew if I didn't do it, someone else would. But I was worried. What if I failed and made a fool of myself?

I picked up the phone and called performance, nutrition and physiology expert Dr Justin Roberts. He was a lecturer at the University of Hertfordshire and had worked with top athletes at the British Olympic Medical

Centre. He had also advised the England Senior Men's Football team on ways to improve their performance. He had helped me and the Pink Lady PoleCats as we trained for the Polar Challenge, so he knew what I was capable of. 'Can you see yourself standing on the summit of Everest?' he asked me. 'Yes, I can,' was my honest reply. I really could see myself doing this. I believed I could do it. 'Then that's the first crucial step,' replied Justin.

My mind was made up. Maybe it was possible to achieve the unthinkable.

I was apprehensive but also excited.

Ben was thrilled when I agreed to join him on the climb. We were going to embark on this adventure together. But we knew it was not going to be easy.

We began to put a plan together. We sought advice from people who had already reached the summit. Ben sent a message to all his fellow students and lecturers at the London Business School looking for other climbers to join our team, and Greg Maud and Omar Samara replied. Greg was a 32-year-old long-distance runner who had previously trekked to Everest Base Camp and had a dream to reach the summit. He was working for one of the world's largest mining companies and had a wife and young son back home in South Africa. Omar was twenty-eight and had grown up in Egypt. The first time he had seen snow was when he was sixteen. He wanted to be the first Egyptian to reach the summit.

With our team complete we set a date for April 2007. April, we discovered, was the best month to attempt the summit as there is a gap in the weather before the monsoon season moves in and the 100 mph winds make the climb impossible.

We had just eighteen months to prepare and so much to do. Dr Roberts helped us draw up a physical and mental training programme, but there were so many other things to consider. We needed an experienced guide to lead us, we needed permits, and we needed money and lots of advice. Ben arranged a meeting with the man who would eventually lead our expedition, Kenton Cool, while I met with Paul Deegan, a mountaineer who had climbed to the summit of Everest. With his vast experience Paul was able to give us first-hand advice on the type of clothing, equipment and food we needed and where to source it and the level of commitment we needed to put into our preparation and training schedule. He also explained the pros and cons of climbing with or without oxygen and the dangers of altitude sickness.

The choice of whether to use oxygen is debated time and time again. Sir Edmund Hillary and Tenzing Norgay used very basic oxygen systems in 1953 when they reached the top. In 1978, when Reinhold Messner became the first person to climb to the summit without extra oxygen, he proved what some doctors and specialists thought impossible, that humans could survive breathing thin air. But he was an extremely experienced mountaineer and our team, who were making their first attempt, would need extra oxygen to help us breathe in the thin air. The effects of the extreme height were my biggest concerns, because I did not know how my body would react. Your level of fitness is not an indicator of how you will react and it's not possible to do any tests that will gauge your ability to acclimatise. The highest I had climbed was 4,167 m to the top of Jebel Toubkal in Morocco.

'The biggest danger is Acute Mountain Sickness, or AMS,' Paul explained. 'It's the body's reaction to a lack of oxygen and leads to headaches and nausea, loss of appetite and difficulty sleeping. That's why it's important to take your time and control your climbing to no more than 400 m per day so that your body can become accustomed to the new conditions.

'If climbers and trekkers miss the early symptoms of AMS and continue climbing then it can be serious,' he warned. 'Fluid can gather in the lungs and brain and that can be life-threatening. The only remedy is to get off the mountain and into hospital. Depending on where this happens you may have to rely on your team mates to carry you down the mountain as it's impossible to get a rescue helicopter above Base Camp. And that in itself can be dangerous.'

It was a lot to take in, but Ben and I knew that these things were important if we were going to succeed in reaching the top of Everest safely.

Our next meeting was with our potential guide, Kenton Cool. If ever there was a guy who lived up to his name, it was Kenton. A tall, angular Brit, he had a reputation for being one of the most daring and successful climbers. He had already reached the summit three times and had a hundred per cent success rate for getting his climbers to the top of the world.

He gave us a checklist which we had to complete before he would even consider taking us. What climbing experience did we have? Did we have cold weather experience? What was the longest expedition we had completed? Would we be fit enough?

Having experienced eighteen days in the Arctic, I was confident that I could live for two months in sub-zero temperatures in a tent in the Himalayas. My climbing skills needed to be stronger but speaking to other mountain leaders I had climbed with, I knew I could improve these over time. Our overall levels of fitness were good and our work with Dr Roberts proved we were serious.

But the big question mark was altitude. 'How high have you climbed?' Kenton wanted to know. 'You need to have climbed an 8,000 m mountain before considering Everest,' he advised. So it was agreed that we would set a goal to climb the sixth highest mountain in the world, Cho Oyu. Standing at 8,201 m high it was also in the Himalayas, just thirty miles away from Everest. If we could succeed on Cho Oyu, it would be our gateway to Everest.

Chapter Three

PREPARING FOR EVEREST

Ben, Greg, Omar and I focussed on getting ready for the enormous challenge we had set ourselves. Already the expedition was starting to dominate our lives. I thought that the training schedule for the Polar Challenge had been intense, but Everest was punishing. I declined invitations to parties, spent less time with friends and family and made sure that I was doing everything I could to be in the best shape for the expedition. A half-hearted attempt simply wasn't good enough for me, it was all or nothing ... and I loved it.

Our coach, Dr Roberts, put us through an initial fitness test. We were put on a treadmill and hooked up to machines which tested our heart rates and the amount of oxygen our bodies used while exercising. 'If you want to make it to the summit, you will need to be lean and as fit as a top athlete,' he explained. 'I want to give you the best possible chance of reaching your goal.' He produced a strict diet and exercise regime for us which, if we followed it, would increase our fitness, strength and stamina.

Our diet was based on eating healthy foods, lots of vegetables, fruit, porridge and chicken, which released energy slowly to feed your brain, muscles and body, while avoiding sugary things like Mars Bars, chocolate chip cookies and alcohol. It was hard at first. Mondays to Fridays were usually spent in the gym. Some days I would be weightlifting and at other times interval training on the treadmill, alternating speeds between 8 kmph and 12 kmph, pushing my body hard.

It was painful but necessary. My favourite exercise was balancing on a wobble board to improve my footing ready for climbing across icy crevasses on ladders on Everest. At first I could barely manage to stay upright for ten seconds, but over time I built up to five minutes.

Living in the middle of London was not the best place for training but we made the most of it by running 13-mile half marathons around the centre of the city following the Regent's Canal and taking in the sights from Hyde Park to the Houses of Parliament. Fridays were the only times we allowed ourselves to relax and have a well-deserved beer. As the months went on and we became more single-minded about our regime even the Friday beer stopped.

Weekends were mostly spent under canvas as we trained in the Brecon Beacons, Snowdonia or the Lake or Peak Districts. We would arrive late in the evening on a Friday night and instead of putting up our tent and relaxing, we would pick up our heavy rucksacks and hike late into the night, stopping to pitch camp in the cold and total darkness. We kept pushing ourselves, walking up to seventeen hours a day, knowing we would need to be able to endure such tiredness to reach the camps on our way to the top of Cho Oyu and then Everest.

Even holidays were spent on mountains. Critical to our training were trips to places where we could test ourselves at high altitude. I travelled to France to climb Europe's highest mountain, Mont Blanc, and together with Ben and Omar I climbed Mount Kilimanjaro, the highest peak in Africa. Every trip was designed to get us closer to our goal.

When we weren't being challenged physically, we had to use our brains to figure out ways of finding enough money to make our dreams come true. We might be able to achieve the peak of our fitness, but if we didn't have

£54,000 each to fund our journey to the summit, it was never going to happen. We needed over £25,000 to pay for our guides and all the permits, travel costs and equipment we would need to take up Everest. Our training trips to Cho Oyu, France and Africa were also costly. There was a long list of almost a hundred specialist items of warm clothing and equipment we would need to take with us on both mountains. Specialist sleeping bags which would keep us warm at temperatures below −40°C cost more than £500 each. The all-in-one down suits which I had been advised were essential to wear at all times at the higher camps on Everest would cost up to £1,000 apiece. Even the insulated mittens and boots we would need were hundreds of pounds. It would all mount up.

'We're each going to need to find sponsors,' said Ben. 'I'll start working on a website and brochure which we can all use to showcase our expedition and attract sponsors.' I set about organising events, compiling lists of potential sponsors and drafting the first of what would be hundreds of letters, highlighting the fact that I would make history as the first Welsh woman to reach the summit. I felt confident that I would get a positive response. I could show a previous track record of achievement in extreme environments and I was ready for the next challenge.

Friends and colleagues were incredibly helpful and made numerous introductions for us, some even suggesting brands or products which might support us. 'Have you thought of Persil Small & Mighty washing detergent?' one friend joked. But despite some good suggestions and a lot of creativity, actually securing financial support was difficult.

Our friends' and families' generous offerings of £50 here and £100 there were touching, but were not going to get us anywhere near our target. Many outdoor-gear companies offered us free goods, which was fantastic, but we still needed cash.

As the rejection letters flooded in, I started to question whether we would ever achieve our dream. I was feeling the stress. I realised that many major companies were sceptical about being associated with such a dangerous expedition. The statistics did not make our task any easier; you frequently read that one in ten expeditions ended in tragedy and I guessed that businesses were reluctant to be involved in anything that might bring negative publicity.

I also learnt that being Welsh and living outside Wales was not a benefit to our cause. I wondered if companies in Wales didn't care because I lived in England, and the businesses in London didn't care that I was Welsh. I even applied to a national women's magazine, which was giving out a £25,000 bursary to help a woman achieve her dream. I got down to the final four but didn't win it. Naturally I was deflated, but the team couldn't allow all of this disappointment to drain our enthusiasm.

How could we convince people that we were determined? We had committed all our savings to climb Cho Oyu in October 2006, not knowing if we would ever have the funds to go to Everest.

When a huge box from one of our equipment sponsors, Mountain Hardware, arrived at our house, I was as excited as a kid at Christmas. Inside were fleeces, down jackets, gloves, mittens, windproof trousers, jackets and the all-important –40°C sleeping bags which we needed for the expedition. Cotswold Outdoor also sent us essential items of kit, including technical watches which recorded how high you were on the mountain. And DMM, a climbing equipment company in north Wales, supplied us with hardware like crampons, ropes, carabiners – the hooks climbers use to attach themselves to ropes, and ice axes. At least the outdoor world had faith in us.

Before leaving for the Cho Oyu expedition in Tibet I left my job at British Exploring. I had loved my three years there, made many friends, and been given some amazing opportunities. But I had to focus on this challenge full time. I'd already used up all my holidays, and now I needed another six weeks to attempt Cho Oyu. It was a sad day when I handed my notice in.

Climbing Cho Oyu was an enormous challenge on its own, but it was an important step on our mission to reach Everest. Arriving in the Himalayas for the first time I was amazed by what I saw – it was simply breathtaking. The Himalayas is home to many of the world's highest peaks and from where we stood in Tibet it stretched for 2,500 km. It was hard to take in its sheer scale: hundreds of snow-capped, ice-encrusted, jagged peaks reaching up more than 7,000 m towards the sky, each commanding respect. Suddenly I felt very small and insignificant and I was apprehensive about the climb.

It was my first experience of climbing at high altitude and in thin air and I suffered daily headaches. During the climb I seriously considered turning around and going home. My head hurt so much I had to lie down in a tent. My eyes were sensitive to light and I had completely lost my appetite.

I wanted to cry. To turn around now would be failure and would kill any hope of ever reaching the summit of Everest. I needed to be successful and so I took my time and waited patiently for my body to adapt. After five weeks we finally made our push for the summit and the all-important climb above 8,000 m. Unfortunately, Ben's attempt ended at 7,000 m when he developed a black spot in his vision caused by the lack of oxygen and had to turn back. Omar, who was recovering from glandular fever, was also forced to turn back at that point, leaving me and my Sherpa, Lhakpa Tundu, to make it to the top without them.

Standing on the summit of Cho Oyu, which was much flatter than I had expected, I stared out across the ragged spires of black rock and ice which made up the other mountain peaks. There in the distance Everest, the Mother Mountain, stood tall and majestic. A ring of wispy, white clouds formed a halo around her summit. I gazed into the bright sunshine trying to recognise the familiar areas I had so far only read about. From miles away I could make out the ridge line of Everest and the rock faces of Lhotse and Nuptse, which cut across the blue skyline. I traced a path with my eyes up from the Western Cwm to the South Col and pictured myself making my way up towards the summit. I felt as if I could almost reach out and touch it.

'I've managed it this far. I can definitely get to the summit of Everest,' I said to myself, determined we would get to Everest at all costs.

When we got back home I threw myself into finding that elusive sponsor with more determination than ever. There could be no turning back. We had to find the money. We worked hard to create packages that would attract the right sponsor. We organised a black-tie ball which helped to raise thousands of pounds towards our target. But a month before we were due to leave for Everest we still did not have enough money. In desperation I turned to my parents to borrow money. It was a last resort, knowing that if I didn't succeed I would have the added stress of paying back this loan, with nothing to show for it.

Then, with only one week to go before our departure, we were approached by two companies who wanted to be a part of the expedition. Our persistence had paid off. Both Investec Asset Management and Find.co.uk employed graduates of the London Business School, where Omar and Ben were studying, and could see the potential in our team. With their sponsorship we reached our target. Now there was nothing to stop us trying to achieve our goal.

Chapter Four

JOURNEY TO NEPAL

The day of our departure for Everest arrived. I've never been fond of saying goodbye, but as I stood at the gate at London's Heathrow Airport, preparing to board the plane, I felt sadness wash over me. As I hugged Mum, Dad and my sister Olivia, I wondered would I return a heroine; or would I perish on the world's highest mountain? There was no way of knowing. Physically I was prepared, but my fate was in the hands of Mother Nature. I couldn't let my nerves show to my family. They had their own worries to deal with.

I kissed my family goodbye. 'Keep yourself safe,' Dad whispered as I turned with the rest of the team to go through to the departure lounge. On the plane, I lost control and broke down in tears, and for an hour I sobbed quietly. For the first time on this great adventure I was truly worried about what lay ahead. I looked across to Ben, who also looked upset. In his hand he was holding a letter which read 'I'm just writing to say how much your dad and I love you. Don't do anything stupid. Keep safe until we see you again. We love you so much. Mum xxxx.'

It was a long and emotional journey but eventually we arrived in Kathmandu, the capital city of Nepal and the place where all Everest expeditions begin. Situated in a valley, with the huge peaks of Everest and its sister mountains barely visible in the distance, Kathmandu is a real melting pot of western tourism and eastern spiritual traditions. Some guide books say there are more temples than houses and more gods than people. The majority of local people follow either the Hindu or Buddhist religions.

The air was heavy with the buzz of beeping motorcycles, the shouts from street traders selling their fake outdoor gear and souvenirs, and the bells of the rickshaw cyclists mixed with the smells from the food sellers, whose meat and fish stalls gave off stale odours, attracting flies and passing dogs. We had been here six months earlier on our venture to Cho Oyu, and nothing had changed. If anything it felt more frantic.

We had just two days to gather together all our kit and test our communications equipment in preparation for our expedition. Much of our bulky equipment, such as our sleeping bags, padded jackets, crampons, socks and carabiners, had been left in storage in blue plastic barrels in the basement of our expedition guiding company in Kathmandu following our Cho Oyu expedition.

'I just hope that mice haven't got in and eaten my down suit,' I said to Ben. A down suit is the most important and most expensive single item needed for expeditions and mine had been specially made. It was a relief to find my suit was safely stored when we finally opened up our barrels and checked the contents.

We left Kathmandu to fly up to Lukla, the town where most people start their treks to Everest Base Camp. I had read that Lukla Airport was rated the smallest and 'most dangerous airport in the world'. And from the photographs I had seen of the runway, which ran downhill to the mountain's edge and a 2,000 m drop into the valley below, I was not going to dispute that fact. Perched on the edge of a mountain, only small, fixed-wing aircraft were able to land.

'That's not a plane, that's a food mixer,' Ben muttered to me as we approached the 26-seater plane that was to carry us up into the mountains. It had a single propeller above each wing and looked rather flimsy.

'I hope it's not windy up there,' I replied. I had visions of the slightest gust blowing the tiny aircraft into the mountains. The sun was shining as we sat on the airport runway but conditions often changed dramatically to cloud, high winds and heavy rain at higher altitudes.

We took our seats, tightened our seat belts, balanced our carefully packed rucksacks on our laps and prepared for take-off. Twenty minutes later we were being carefully navigated through the steep-sided valleys and tree-covered slopes of the Khumbu valley. It was a tense journey but far easier than trekking, a journey which the explorers in the 1950s took a month to cover.

Lukla was the starting point of our trek to Everest Base Camp. The journey would take us eleven days, stopping off at traditional Nepalese tea houses along the way. The route to Base Camp is popular with trekking tourists. On this part of the trip our team included a group of friends and colleagues, who were also making the trek to Base Camp to raise money for our chosen charity, the Prince's Trust. For the first few days we walked along footpaths which were rugged and rocky, and it reminded me of being back home on the Pembrokeshire Coast Path. The landscape was green and vibrant in the valley and the sun was so hot we were able to walk in just shorts and T-shirts. It was all very relaxed and casual, crossing rope bridges strung over deep river gorges. Our porters had gone ahead of us, carrying most of our bulky equipment, leaving us to carry our personal items in a rucksack. We met up with them later for our overnight stops at various tea houses.

The tea houses, as their name suggests, were primitive cafés which served hot, dark Nepalese tea and local dishes of dumplings and noodles to weary travellers. Their main source of heat came from yak dung, which was burnt in the fire pit, and was responsible for the rather unpleasant odour which seemed to seep into the walls and your clothes. After a long day trekking we were often too tired to care.

As we walked we met many people from all over the world whose goal was to make it to Everest Base Camp. We also discovered the unwritten rule of the footpath was to give way to yaks. The paths up and down the mountain were dotted with the great shaggy-haired, cow-like animals, which the local guides used to carry supplies and equipment up to Base Camp.

They were pretty stubborn and their long horns meant there was no question of who would give way first!

Of all the places we visited along the way, Namche Bazaar was the busiest. Halfway along the path, it is the hub of Sherpa society. Sherpas are the mountain people who live high in the Himalayan mountains. For generations they lived a simple, hardy life up there but now many of the families earn a living from tourism and the visitors to Everest. The most experienced Sherpa mountain climbers are highly respected and can earn thousands of pounds by leaving their families for two months at a time, risking their lives to lead expeditions to the summit. Ever since Sherpa Tenzing accompanied Sir Edmund Hillary, Sherpas have provided their services to hundreds of international climbers. Tragically, many have lost their lives on the mountain. Before we left Britain I had read about the achievements of Sherpa Pasang Lhamu, who was the first female to reach the summit fourteen years before me, but who died during her descent. It was a reminder that Everest had no respect, even for her own.

Closer to Base Camp we stopped beside tombstones, lasting memorials to climbers who had been killed on the mountain, and passed the wreckage of a helicopter, which had been caught in an up-draught and dragged into the glacier two years earlier and was now encased in the ice. Helicopters are unable to fly above Base Camp, which is one of the reasons why climbers who fall to their death climbing Everest are often left in their icy tombs on the mountain as it's impossible to get help in by air. It was a chilling reminder of the fragile and dangerous world we were about to enter.

Chapter Five

AT BASE CAMP

We arrived at Everest Base Camp on 9 April, a day ahead of schedule. Base Camp is the ultimate destination for thousands of trekkers each year, but for us, this was just the beginning.

Looking across to the summit, suddenly I felt butterflies in my stomach. I was intimidated by its size and scale. I tilted my head back and squinted high into the sky, trying to focus on every minute detail of the route we would be following, picking out the famous features of the Hillary Step close to the top. 'How can anyone ever climb that high?' I asked myself, wondering at the achievement of the explorers who had been the first to adventure so high. Snowdonia seemed as flat as a car park in comparison. I questioned whether I had challenged myself too far. There did not appear to be an obvious route, but I reminded myself how mountains are frequently deceptive.

The Base Camp set-up itself was pretty impressive. Nestled among the dips and ridges of the Khumbu Glacier, it was a sea of grey and rugged glacier rocks. Being 5,380 m above sea level there are no plants or trees, and the only colour breaking up this monochrome landscape were the mishmash of blue, yellow and red dome-shaped tents and strings of multi-coloured prayer flags.

Up until the mid 1990s, Base Camp had been a very different scene and rightly earned its reputation as a high altitude rubbish tip – climbers attempting Everest would leave all their tin cans, food wrappers and even human waste there. But following massive clean-ups, one of which was led by our mountaineering advisor Paul Deegan, the camp is now clean and expeditions are obliged to carry all their rubbish, even human waste, back down the valley in barrels.

At any one time there can be up to four hundred people staying at this basic and barren campsite. Not all of these people will climb to the summit. It is the base for expedition back-up teams, porters, Sherpas, cooks and medical support staff. I was surprised to see a sign for a bakery, offering breads, cakes and back-rubs. It seemed that there was good business in baking at high altitude and their apple pie was the best I've ever tasted.

At Base Camp we said goodbye to our friends in the trekking group, who had reached their goal, raised their money for the Prince's Trust, and could now go back home to their families and friends. They had made us laugh, helped us to relax and made us believe we could reach the summit. We would miss them.

Before they left one lady donated me some vital equipment: a hairbrush to replace mine, which had snapped in the cold, and some face cream. 'If you do have a rare chance to wash your hair, at least it won't be a mass of tangles afterwards,' she thoughtfully said. The idea of having a shower seemed like a distant dream. Showers would be rare. To have a shower meant melting snow and heating it to lukewarm. The fuel supplies our team of porters had carried up to camp were limited and needed to be saved for cooking our meals and hot drinks. If we were lucky we would have a shower once every ten days.

Each expedition team had its own base set-up at camp, complete with a mess tent and kitchen staffed by locals to feed its guides, porters and climbers. It was here we met up with our expedition leader, Kenton Cool, his assistant, Rob Casserley, and our Base Camp manager Henry Todd. It was Todd's job to manage the timing of our ascents, control communications on the mountain, monitor the weather, appoint our climbing Sherpas and make sure we had everything we needed, including oxygen for the final push.

Todd was a charming character and had a great reputation for getting climbers to the summit of Everest. Kenton also had an amazing reputation among climbers, and had worked with Sir Ranulph Fiennes. He had broken many mountaineering records. He walked with a slight limp as a result of a serious accident when he fell climbing a slate quarry in Snowdonia. 'What doesn't kill you makes you stronger,' he once said. His assistant, Rob Casserley, was a surgeon and experienced high-altitude mountaineer, who had starred in the BBC documentary *Everest ER* about medicine and climbing on Everest.

By day Base Camp had something of a sixth-form common-room atmosphere as everyone in the group became better acquainted. Some were wealthy professionals who were fulfilling their dreams; others like Rob were there to work. Our group included Rob's girlfriend Anna Shekhdar, who was an Accident and Emergency consultant from Bristol. We immediately struck up a bond as we were the only British women in our expedition group and we had both been persuaded to make this journey by our boyfriends. Added to the mix was a climber from Kent called Mike, who was making a second attempt on Everest having lost a team member in an accident on an expedition a few years earlier; Pat, a male nurse from Canada who was carrying his friend's ashes in his rucksack which he intended to scatter from the summit; and Bo from Michigan who worked in real estate, and who I first met when climbing Cho Oyu. The American group also included Sam, an eighteen-year-old who, in accompanying her doctor dad and helping make his dream come true, was also aiming to become the youngest female American to reach the summit.

The mess tent at camp became a focal point for our group. Food was important to the climbers for sustaining energy levels as our bodies started to get used to the lack of oxygen. Mealtimes would be spent in the mess tent, dining on traditional Tibetan dishes like rice, noodles, soup and a spicy lentil dish called dahl, as well as more familiar meals of eggs, porridge and rice pudding. The real delicacies were popcorn and Pringles, which soon became a staple of our diet. My favourite meal was Easiyo, powdered yoghurt, which might sound disgusting, but was delicious.

Vitamins were also essential to make up for the lack in our camp diet. I followed the advice of our nutritionist Dr Roberts and made sure I took the necessary supplements, a total of nine tablets each day. Food hygiene was also important to prevent the spread of stomach bugs. Rob was constantly reminding members of the group, 'Do not leave the spoon in the coffee jar. You could have germs on your hands. Those germs are left on the spoon and can pass onto the coffee. The next person to make a cup of coffee picks up those germs. You've all trained hard and spent a lot of time, effort and money to get this far. Do you want to end your expedition because of careless bugs?'

Toilet facilities consisted of a barrel sunk into the ground. It had been carefully constructed with rocks around the edge of the hole and a toilet seat on legs. I soon found that the best technique was to squat and get out as quickly as possible. As we ventured further up the mountain I would learn to accept this toilet as relative luxury because at higher camps there was no tent, no barrel and no privacy.

Despite the harsh, primitive conditions there was a great spirit of fun among the expedition at Base Camp. In the mess tent we had set up a communication centre, which consisted of a sturdy computer and a satellite link to the internet. Using this, we were able to write a daily blog to update our friends and followers on our achievements.

The first night at Base Camp Ben and I retired to our two-man tent and snuggled into our sleeping bags. Suddenly I was woken by a loud crack, which shook me through my sleeping mat.

'What's happening?' I whispered across to Ben, fearing a rock fall.

'It's only the ice cracking,' he assured me. 'After all, we are camping on a glacier.'

At camp I began to appreciate that climbing the highest mountain in the world would need patience and respect. In this thinning air even the 50 m walk from our tent to the mess tent was hard work and I was shocked by how breathless I felt. It was a sharp reminder of the difficulties we would face further up the climb. The plan was to spend four days at the camp to allow our bodies time to get used to the lack of oxygen before the next part of our journey. We sat down with Kenton, who talked us through what lay ahead.

'You're probably feeling the effects of the altitude already and this is only going to get worse as we climb higher and the oxygen levels decrease,' he reminded us. 'Be patient, your body will naturally attempt to make more red blood cells to stop you feeling so tired and breathless.'

He explained how, over the next couple of weeks, we would do this by making gradual climbs to each of the three camps at higher levels, before returning to Base Camp to rest. Then, when our bodies were ready, we would wait for the right weather before attempting the summit. We would be following the South Col Route taken by Sir Edmund Hillary and Sherpa Tenzing in 1953.

Before leaving we were given a blessing as part of our 'puja' ceremony. The puja is a traditional Buddhist ritual to bless all climbers attempting to climb what the local Nepalese people call Sagarmatha, which means 'goddess of the sky'. The Nepalese are holy people and the prayers and offerings to Buddha are part of their daily rituals at home. On the mountain our party of climbers, guides and porters sat out in the afternoon sun in front of an altar where the offerings of yaks' milk and tsampa, a local food which looked and tasted like sweet, doughy dumplings, were laid out. The prayer flags, which we had seen fluttering from poles at monasteries further down the valley and at various points on our way up the mountain, were hung out by our guides to bless the mountain. Each flag was a coloured rectangle of cotton, with each colour representing the elements: blue for sky, white for wind, red for fire, green for water and yellow for earth. Some had prayers printed on them and as the wind blew the flags, the prayers were scattered into the air. One by one we each knelt before the offerings, our hands together in prayer, as we bowed and chanted to Buddha.

The ceremony was a chance to calmly contemplate what lay ahead. I was relaxed but eager to get going.

Chapter Six

THE ICEFALL

Friday 13 April arrived, the morning of our first climb. I set my alarm for 4.45 a.m. and reminded myself that my granddad Claude always considered the 13th as a 'lucky' day, otherwise I might have let superstition get the better of me. As it was I slept through my alarm and woke up twenty-five minutes late, which left me with just twenty minutes to get ready.

I got up and picked my way across the boulders to the mess tent and forced down a bowl of porridge. With a hearty breakfast inside me, I was ready to face our first nerve-wracking experience. I returned to my tent to collect my rucksack, which I had already packed the night before, and headed to the other side of Base Camp where Kenton, Ben, Greg, Omar and the rest of the team were assembled at the foot of the Icefall.

One of the most dangerous stages of the climb, the Icefall is a jagged mass of ice moving downhill under its own weight. It is estimated that it moves about one metre down the mountain every day. Because of this constant motion, it is notoriously unstable and has claimed the lives of many climbers and Sherpas. Giant crevasses can open up at any second without warning and drag climbers to their death. Seracs, which are huge blocks of ice the size of cars or even houses, have been known to fall and crush climbers under their weight.

Describing his first attempt to climb in 1953, Edmund Hillary later confessed in his memoir *High Adventure*, 'I didn't like the place at all and felt we shouldn't be there.' I could understand his awe and fear for even though I had seen photographs and been warned by other climbers, nothing had prepared me for its sheer size.

At the start of every season a team of Sherpas, affectionately known as the Ice Doctors, are employed to create a path through the valley of ice. It's their job to anchor the ropes and ladders for climbers to follow. But even these are no guarantee of safety. In this high-rise maze of ice, every step was uncertain. Since leaving home, I had been dreading the ladder crossings in the Icefall. I had seen films of climbers carefully picking their way over light ladders slung across wide crevasses, the ladders moving under their weight, and it terrified me. While I had been able to prepare for the climbing and sub-zero conditions, there was no way of simulating this experience until we reached the real thing.

An hour into our climb and we reached our first ladder. Greg, Omar and Kenton had all gone ahead. A deep, black crevasse and a thin metal ladder stood between us and the rest of the team.

What if I can't pass this first hurdle? I thought to myself. My Everest dream will be over.

'Don't think about it, I've got you,' I heard Ben shout ahead of me, as he held the ropes tightly to reduce any movement. 'Just put one foot in front of the other.' Shakily I took my first steps, carefully trying to avoid getting my crampon spikes caught in the rungs of the ladder. Don't look down, I kept telling myself, my confidence growing with every step. I tried to focus on my feet to avoid looking down into the black hole that gaped below me. When I reached the other side, where Ben was waiting, I heaved a sigh of relief. It wasn't as bad as I anticipated. Actually it was quite fun ... a bit like being in an adventure playground.

Together Ben and I made a great team, holding the ropes for each other and experimenting with different techniques to find the easiest way of negotiating these icy obstacles, while Greg and Omar just powered through. I took my time. It wasn't a race. I wasn't as strong or as fast as Ben, Greg and Omar, who were all over 6 ft tall, but I was as determined and focused. Along the way I discovered the secret to sustaining enough energy was to eat and drink regularly, but this proved easier said than done, as the effects of altitude meant I didn't feel like eating and even less like drinking cold liquid in freezing conditions.

As we climbed higher into the Icefall, my feet started to freeze. I realised I had chosen the wrong boots. The mountaineering boots, which had served me well in Snowdonia, Scotland and the French Alps, were not warm enough. I forced myself to work harder and move faster just to keep warm and reminded myself that next time I would wear my high altitude boots, which hugged my calves right up to my knees and would keep out the cold.

The Icefall seemed to go on for ever and to make it even harder there was no direct route.

Just as we thought we were getting closer to our high point, the path would take a frustrating turn in the opposite direction to avoid a huge block of ice or an area which was prone to avalanches.

On the way up we identified features and gave them nicknames. The 'football pitch' was a relatively flat area amongst the ice rubble, the 'golf ball', a rounded piece of ice with dimples. These gave us reference points for each climb.

One of these features we called the 'tunnel of love' – a tower of ice had fallen across the path leaving a tunnel beneath it. The shortest route was to pass beneath this collapsed piece of ice, but it was dangerous and anything but romantic! 'That may be a shortcut, but it will fall,' one of our local guides warned us and we chose to take the longer route, taking us on yet another loop.

After more than four hours we had climbed 500 m in height and the lack of oxygen was already beginning to have an effect on our team. Under normal conditions a climb of this distance would take less than an hour but the thin air made it difficult. Ben and Kenton started to complain of headaches caused by the altitude.

'Time to turn around, guys,' said Kenton and we headed back to Base Camp. On the way down we noticed the 'tunnel of love' was no more. It had collapsed into the crevasse, making us more even more aware of the dangers. Back at Base Camp Ben and Kenton immediately returned to their tents to try to get rid of their headaches. It was a huge confidence boost for me to have escaped the headaches this time, and kept up with the others. The reality of climbing Everest is that there is a lot of sitting around doing nothing while your body gets used to the lack of oxygen. During these long days the mess tent at Base Camp became a meeting point for our group and we would gather there between meals to play cards and games. On a sunny day, when solar panels could be used to charge electrical items, there were additional entertainment options. 'At 16.30 the cinema will be showing *Top Gun*,' the American climber announced one afternoon as he produced a portable DVD player from his tent. We started to watch but suddenly the film was interrupted by a loud roar in the distance. Looking towards the Icefall we could see clouds of snow cascading down the mountain. 'Avalanche,' Rob warned. Each one of us sitting around the DVD player shuddered as we thought how we would soon be going back up the mountain over that dangerous and unpredictable glacier.

Later that evening, my head also started to feel the effects of the altitude. It was a dull, lingering headache that just wouldn't budge. I took a couple of painkillers and went to bed.

For three days we relaxed at Base Camp. At 6 a.m. on 16 April we entered the Icefall for the second time with the aim of reaching Camp I by late afternoon, where we would spend our first night at higher altitude. As we set off, picking our way up the ice, I felt fit and alert. Before we left I had gone to the mess tent and filled my water bladder with hot water mixed with a summer-fruit-flavoured isotonic high-energy drink. I could feel its heat radiating through my rucksack making me nice and warm and encouraging me to drink.

Having already climbed the first half of the Icefall three days earlier we were on familiar territory and started off at a reasonably quick pace. The ladder bridges were no longer an obstacle. Unfortunately, my energetic mood was soon drained by the lack of oxygen. Climbing amongst the icy blocks and ridges, Ben and I started to feel breathless and stopped to catch our breath and refuel with an energy bar and water. Kenton, Greg and Omar stormed ahead, seemingly unaware of the frosty mountains in our path, leaving Ben and me to bring up the rear where we maintained a steady pace, stopping every hour to refill our bodies with water and snacks.

The last few hours of the climb to Camp I were tedious. We eventually reached the top of the Icefall and heaved a sigh of relief as a white, seemingly flat plateau stretched out ahead of us. But this was Everest and nothing was as straightforward as it first appeared. 'Watch out for snow bridges,' Kenton warned us, pointing ahead to what seemed like a low ridge of driven snow breaking the flatness of the white plain. 'That's where the snow has blown over a deep crevasse. You can't always see them. Just because it's flat don't think you don't need to clip on to the ropes. If you stand on a snow bridge without a rope, you're gone.'

Walking in the open valley, there was little shelter from the midday sunshine, which was reaching temperatures of up to 30 degrees. It may sound odd, but here we were in the middle of a snowy wilderness and we had to pause in the shade of a large block of ice and scoop up handfuls of snow to rub into our foreheads to stop us overheating in the bright sun.

We had been walking for almost eight hours; up ahead over the furthest ridge we could see a cluster of tents. 'We're still nowhere near,' Ben said, exhausted and frustrated by the constant, tedious, zigzagging route we had to negotiate. We pressed on. We had no choice, there was no turning back. Then, as we turned another corner, there, much to our relief was Camp I, laid out like the peaks and troughs of waves on the ocean. Each expedition had pitched its tents on a different peak and there was pressure on the Sherpa teams to get to camp first and choose the best locations. Omar and Greg were sharing a tent, I was sharing with Ben and Kenton had one to himself. Outside the weather was variable. When the sun was out it was too hot, but when it went in we were plunged back into minus temperatures. The tent offered a consistent warm temperature. Despite it being only 2.30 p.m., we took off our harnesses and crampons and crawled inside and lit the gas stove. For dinner that evening we ate tinned pâté and biscuits, followed by a plate of Dolmio-filled pasta and stir-in sauce, washed down with plenty of hot black Nepalese tea.

By 6 p.m. I was exhausted. I could hardly keep my eyes open. I could feel a headache creeping up, so I again took a couple of painkillers, which I carried in my rucksack, then filled my water bladder with hot water to act as a hot-water bottle and climbed into my sleeping bag for the night.

Getting ready for sleep on Everest had its own uncomfortable set of rituals. We could not simply jump into a nice warm bed after a long day of exhausting ice climbing. We were sleeping on a sheet of ice. We had an insulated sleeping mat separating our sleeping bags from the icy floor but as soon as you set a foot off the mat, the cold penetrated deep into your body. Our extra-warm sleeping bags were essential but they were also freezing cold. The trick was to strip down to one layer of thermal leggings, a long-sleeved vest, socks and gloves, then jog on the spot before getting into our sleeping bags. This had the effect of raising our heart rate and pumping more blood around our bodies to warm us up.

The other big problem was toilet facilities. It's bad enough waking up in the middle of the night at home in a cold bedroom wanting a wee. But on Everest it meant leaving the protection of your sleeping bag, then in the pitch black of night putting on your boots and crampons to stop you slipping on the ice, then exposing your body to the dangerously cold weather outside to walk to a barrel in the ground. It was safer to stay in your sleeping bag and reach out for a wide-necked bottle!

At night the wind was unsettling. One minute there would be complete silence, the next a huge gust of wind would blow and rearrange our belongings inside the tent.

The following morning we ventured a little further towards Camp II, before returning back down the Icefall. I was reminded of a book I had read before we left the UK. Of all the first-person accounts of climbing Everest, *Into Thin Air* was probably the worst choice of reading material. It told the true story of Everest's worst disasters which happened in May 1996. Eight climbers belonging to three separate expeditions, caught in a storm and hurricane-force winds, lost their way down and died of exposure and the effects of altitude, all within twenty-four hours. The writer, Jon Krakauer, a veteran American journalist and seasoned climber who had been sent on the expedition to report for an American climbing magazine, survived to tell the story. But his guide, the celebrated Everest guide Rob Hall, was among those killed.

'Each trip through the Icefall was a little like playing a round of Russian roulette,' Krakauer wrote. 'Sooner or later any given serac was going to fall over without warning, and you could only hope you weren't beneath it when it toppled. Since the Icefall's first victim in 1963, eighteen other climbers had died here.'

As we descended through the icy maze towards Base Camp I stopped in fright as the ground shook under me and a booming sound echoed through the valley. 'Ben!' I shouted out, as he was hidden behind a boulder of ice. 'Are you OK, what was that?'

Ben came rushing back into sight. 'A serac has fallen further up the Icefall. Let's get out of here,' he said.

Chapter Seven

APPROACHING THE DEATH ZONE

The final stage of our preparation for the summit was to spend a night at Camp III. Teetering dangerously at 7,100 m up the mountain on the edge of a wall of ice known as the Lhotse Face, it was just outside the Death Zone, and the last camp where we would be able to spend a night before returning to Base Camp to rest and prepare for our final push.

Although Camp IV was only 1,000 m higher, it fell within the critical 8,000 m Death Zone where the level of oxygen in the air drops dramatically below one third of that at sea level and temperatures plummet even lower, increasing the risk of frostbite. At this height it is almost impossible to survive without extra oxygen. We would only camp here when we knew we were ready to make our attempt on the summit.

It was a cold but beautiful clear morning as we left Camp II to climb to the foot of the Lhotse Face. Undulating fields of snow spread out to our right and on the left pinnacles of ice rose out of the ground. As usual I was careful to pace myself at the start, stopping regularly to drink and snack on high-energy bars. I knew that once we started climbing the icy face it would be difficult to stoke up until we reached the top and I wanted to make sure I had as much energy as possible.

The Lhotse Face was the key to the summit for Edmund Hillary's expedition in 1953. In the half a century that had followed, many climbers had ventured up its sheer wall. It had also claimed the lives of more than twenty climbers. It was a daunting prospect – a 1,000 m sheer wall of rock and ice and it stood between us and Camp III.

As we approached the face we saw an Italian climber who was visibly upset; something had gone wrong.

'Stay where you are, I'm going to find out what's going on,' Kenton told us as he walked to meet the lost climber. Just out of view lay the body of a Sherpa guide. He had been leading the Italian man up the Lhotse Face when a block of ice fell down striking him full in the face. He had lost his grip on the ice and fallen to his death.

This close brush with death raised the question, should we carry on? It's a fact of Everest that you are never far away from a dead body. I had heard many ghoulish stories from adventurers who had seen hands or legs sticking out of snow drifts on their way to the summit. Fortunately I had not witnessed such sights and neither did I want to. But this encounter with death was too close. We were all shaken by what we had nearly witnessed and called a crisis meeting with Kenton. 'I don't want to go any further,' I said, choking back my tears. I was all for heading back down the Icefall to Base Camp, getting my belongings and leaving Nepal.

'It's just too dangerous,' Ben agreed. 'If we had set out thirty minutes earlier this morning it could have been any one of us in the path of that ice block.'

'It's your call,' was Kenton's response. 'I'm not going to force you to do anything you're not comfortable with. But if it's any consolation, there is a question over whether the dead man was clipped on to the ropes.'

It was little comfort to us. 'I don't want to go up there today,' I said, feeling that it would show a lack of respect to the dead man to go on. However, the team were keen to continue and so after some sombre reflection about the incident, and much personal questioning about why we were there when the dangers were so real, we continued up the face.

We climbed higher, digging our crampons into the ice, paying even closer attention to how securely we clipped ourselves on to the ropes before hauling our weight up the wall of ice. The thinning air was sapping our energy and each step seemed like an enormous effort. We experimented with taking a series of steps then stopping to regain our breath, or trying to get into a very slow plod. The wind swirled around us, picking up loose snow and ice and blowing it into our faces. After six hours our bright yellow tents at Camp III came into view. But it was not a sight that gave me any relief.

Perched on a narrow ledge, and staked down with heavy ropes to stop the 100 mph winds from ripping them off the mountain's face, our tents looked just like I felt – vulnerable and exposed. It gave me some comfort to know that our Sherpas had succeeded in claiming the location that was least narrow and exposed. Even so, Camp III was horrible. At least on Camp II we were on the relative flat. Here we were on our own, nestling on a cliff face, aware that any wrong move could mean a fall to our death.

Kenton showed us our toilet facilities, the crevasse which ran along the ledge by our tents. 'Don't leave your tent without your crampons or rope – even to use the loo,' he warned us. Thank heavens for bottles, I thought to myself. On the plus side there was the most amazing view from our tent looking down over the vast white expanse of the Western Cwm – the peak of Cho Oyu miles away in the distance.

Cocooned in our tent, tucked up inside my specialist sleeping bag, I was warm and fell into a deep sleep. Outside the icy silence of the mountain was broken only by the noise of the high winds.

Suddenly I woke up in panic, with the feeling that someone had punched me in the chest. But there was no one there. The tent was still intact. Breathless and panting I shook Ben, who was fast asleep in his bag. I gulped for air and tried to stay calm. I had been warned about a phenomenon called Cheyne-Stoking which happened to some people at high altitude where your lungs 'forget to breathe'. I lay in my sleeping bag forcing myself to take deep breaths until I eventually fell back to sleep. I had just experienced my first bout of this and at that point I knew that when we entered the Death Zone things would get even tougher.

Chapter Eight

TO THE SUMMIT?

We returned to Base Camp, satisfied that our time at Camp II and III had been a success. Our bodies were getting more accustomed to the thin Everest air and we were now able to walk around without feeling exhausted. Our next climb up the mountain would be all the way to the summit.

At base, Henry Todd was watching the weather forecasts, looking for a five-day window of settled, clear weather to plan our summit day. But storm clouds were moving in on the Himalayas, making an immediate trip to the summit too dangerous. We hung around Base Camp hoping the weather would pass as quickly as it had arrived. After a couple of days Henry called us together. 'There's no chance of good weather for at least a week,' he said. 'You might as well go back down the valley and wait.'

Ben, Greg, Omar and I trekked back down to the relative luxury of tea house lodgings in Pangboche and waited. By day we went on short walks around the valley and in the evening we sat in the tea house, playing card games and reading to pass the time.

Eventually we got a call from Henry telling us to get back to Base Camp as the weather was looking good for the summit on 17 May.

This was it. We finally had a date for our push to the summit. The pressure was on to stay healthy. We had been in Nepal for almost six weeks and at some point we had all suffered from sickness and diarrhoea caused by the lack of hygiene and change in diet as well as headaches and nausea from the lack of oxygen. Now it was more important than ever to avoid local stomach bugs which could affect our performance.

Arriving back at Base Camp felt like ground-hog day. Our guides and porters were waiting to greet us. We were interviewed by a camera crew from the BBC who were making a documentary on the Himalayan Rescue Association's emergency medical centre at Base Camp. Kenton called us together for a weather meeting. 'The weather forecasts look good for a summit between May 16 and 19. So we will need to leave for Camp II on either May 12 or 13. But nothing is certain and we will be watching as the forecasts become more accurate over the next couple of days and we may have to adjust our plans.'

There was a buzz of nervous excitement among the group as we anticipated touching the roof of the world. Soon we would stand in the footprints of great adventurers like Sir Edmund Hillary, Reinhold Messner, Sir Chris Bonington and Doug Scott. 'I can't believe we're actually going to do it,' I whispered to Ben. In my head I had a vision of me flying my Welsh flag on the summit. In five days I hoped it would be real. I hoped we would be safe.

Back in the tent I concentrated hard on packing my rucksack with my equipment for the climb to the summit. I checked and double-checked that I had everything: ice axe, goggles, fleece layers, energy bars, dry socks, hand and toe warmers and many pairs of gloves. In addition to the essential items were my Welsh flag and my red Welsh rugby shirt. I have always loved the colour red, it's such a cheerful colour, and I wear it as often as I can for sport and outdoor activities. But this jersey had a special importance. The weekend before we left the UK I wore it to watch Wales play England at the Millennium Stadium, Cardiff. Against the odds, Wales won 27–19 and I took this to be a good omen. During half-time a message came over the tannoy. 'Good luck to Tori James. The Welsh Rugby Union would like to wish her every success as she's off to become the first Welsh woman to climb to the top of Everest.' After the match I was presented with a signed flag for the record-breaking journey. I pictured my flag held high on the top of Everest.

On the morning of the start of our summit climb, I woke up at 5 a.m. I should have been excited about the journey ahead, but I felt weak. During night I had started to vomit. This had woken me at intervals and I felt tired. I needed to build up my energy but I couldn't eat anything. Ben, who was also suffering from a similar sickness and diarrhoea, helped. He forced me to drink water with salts which would stop my body from dehydrating.

The climb up to Camp II was a real struggle for both Ben and me. My arms and legs were weak and I felt drained of all my energy. To add to the discomfort the sun was beating down, reflecting fiercely off the snow surfaces and overheating my already fragile body. Great, all I need now is sunstroke to add to my problems, I thought. I dragged myself into our tent at Camp II and lay on the sleeping mat.

Ben handed me a couple of Imodium anti-diarrhoea tablets. Being a doctor's son, Ben had come well prepared with all types of tablets for every possible illness. I took them but they did little to ease my sickness.

Packing my rucksack for the climb to Camp III was a real effort. Normally I would be so precise, but I couldn't be bothered. I was just ramming everything in my bag in a jumble. It was a mess and so was I.

'I can't do this,' I cried to Ben. 'I might be able to make it to Camp III, but unless I make a miracle recovery overnight there's no way I can make it to the top. It needs every bit of concentration and energy I have. And at present I just don't have enough. It will be too dangerous for you and the rest of the team to bring me back down.'

It was a tough decision to make but Ben said, 'I'll come back to Base Camp with you.' Together we broke the news to Kenton as he was preparing to leave with Greg and Omar. The forecast for the top of Everest was looking good. The winds, which had been whipping up snowstorms around the summit, were dropping and it looked like they were going to have sun for their summit day. Everything seemed perfect, which made our illness a real blow.

'It makes sense for you to go back down and stay there until you feel better. We are still in the middle of May, so with any luck there will be other weather windows to make another summit attempt,' Kenton reassured us.

We hugged Greg, Omar and Kenton. 'Good luck. We'll be listening out for you over the radio,' we said, as we headed back down the mountain. At Base Camp I spoke to the doctors within our team who reckoned that I had picked up the dreaded Giardia stomach bug. Giardia is one of the most common germs that strikes down climbers on Everest and is easily spread. 'You might have picked it up in the water or it could have been passed on from someone not washing their hands after using the toilet,' the doctor explained. 'It may have been lying in your stomach for ten days so there was no way to know that you had it when you left Base Camp.' I was relieved it was nothing more serious.

We took medication and waited. At camp it had started to snow. We woke up one morning to the sound of silence. The snow had fallen in the night, covering our tent and belongings under a white fluffy blanket. An eerie stillness was cast over the tents. Digging our way out of our tent, we picked our way through the blizzard to the mess tent to tune into the radio. At that moment Pat (a Canadian climber) walked in and we took one look at him and burst out laughing. He had dressed in the dark and was wearing a pair of underpants on his head. 'Is that a lucky omen?' I asked.

Suddenly the radio crackled to life with Kenton's voice: 'I'm on the summit with Omar and Greg.' We raised a toast of Nepalese tea to our friends. But the celebration was a mix of emotions. I was happy for their success but disappointed that Ben and I were not with them.

Two days later the outlines of three tired figures emerged from the foot of the Icefall and staggered into camp. Ben and I went to Kenton, Greg and Omar. 'Well done, guys,' I cheered, helping Greg to take off his rucksack. I threw my arms around him in celebration and was shocked to feel his bones beneath his padded suit. It had been only four days since we had left them at Camp II, but he looked so gaunt. 'I haven't eaten for days,' he croaked, his voice hoarse from exhaustion.

I turned to congratulate Omar. 'You're the first Egyptian to the summit,' I said with pride.

And as I spoke I could see his eyes were red and bloodshot from the experience. If that's what Everest can do to fit, strong men like Greg and Omar, what chance do I have? I thought.

Chapter Nine

TOP OF THE WORLD

'If you fall, you're dead' was the one thought running though my head as I prepared to leave for the summit of Everest. After months of preparation, the day had finally arrived. Kenton was still predicting good weather for a summit climb on 24 May and I now felt strong.

Ben and I were over the worst of our sickness and had made it back to Camp II. Ben went ahead of me to spend an extra day adjusting at the higher altitude Camp IV. I stayed at Camp II with Kenton, where I rested and listened to various Welsh artists on my MP3 player. The classical arias of Katherine Jenkins, Bryn Terfel and Charlotte Church, mixed with the rock anthems of the Manic Street Preachers and the Stereophonics, reminded me of home and fired me up for the challenge that lay ahead. I wanted to make Wales, my friends, and my family, proud. I thought especially of my late grandparents and hoped they would be watching over me.

I climbed to Camp III with Anna and we shared our fears. We questioned whether we would physically be able to reach the summit. From here we would use oxygen to climb. Kenton handed me an oxygen mask and cylinder. I secured the mask around my face. There was no question about it – we were in extreme conditions. I had practised wearing oxygen masks when we climbed Cho Oyu, but now I was going into the Death Zone, the point where no human life can survive without extra oxygen.

I connected my mask to the cylinder, turned the switch and took my first steps. As soon as the oxygen-rich air hit my lungs, I was off like a train. Being so small, my body was using the oxygen to greater effect and I felt full of energy, turbo-charged. But from here on I was carrying extra weight. Each oxygen tank weighed more than 6 kg and contained enough oxygen to last for only seven or eight hours until we reached Camp IV, where there were additional supplies. I couldn't waste time; the pressure was on to reach the next stage before the oxygen ran out.

Joining other climbers from different expeditions, I made steady progress towards the area known as South Col. The route took us over two distinctive landmarks, the Yellow Band and the Geneva Spur. The golden rock formation of the Yellow Band circled Everest like a giant gold ring while the black, curved rocky edge of the spur stood out in contrast to the whiteness of the surrounding snow-covered landscape.

Having successfully climbed past the spur, we were approaching the top of the Lhotse Face and the air was noticeably thinner. Each step required more energy and concentration. At 2 p.m. we arrived at Camp IV on the South Col, where Ben was already camped and melting snow to make a welcome mug of hot chocolate.

'Are you sure this water is clean?' I asked him as he handed me a mug. It was a well-known fact that climbers at the South Col weren't particular about where they peed.

Sitting in our tent on the South Col camp really felt like we were on the edge of the world. We were almost 3,000 m above Base Camp, looking down onto the rugged peaks and tiny white specks of clouds below.

At 8 p.m. we began to prepare for our final push to the top. I was feeling the fittest I had since we had first arrived at Base Camp. Whether it was the extra oxygen I had been breathing or just the adrenaline rush of excitement, it was a positive sign. I stepped into my down suit and packed two oxygen cylinders in my rucksack. I took my new, unworn, red thermal socks out of their plastic wrapping. I had been careful to keep these socks sealed and fresh as I was paranoid about getting them damp. Any moisture or dampness meant there was a greater risk of a climber's greatest enemy, frostbite. It was hard to tell the difference between having cold toes, and numb flesh which is actually starting to freeze, and I didn't want to risk losing my toes to frostbite.

Underneath my suit I wore three layers: thermal leggings and a long-sleeved vest under fleece trousers and fleece top, and a bulkier fleece jacket. I fixed my goggles and a rubberised neoprene nose cover over my face for protection from the driving wind and snow and picked up my ice axe, which I could use to grip into the ice if I lost my footing.

I attached my oxygen mask over my mouth, switched on my head torch and we were off.

Kenton led the way, followed by Ben and his Sherpa, then me with Sherpa Lhakpa Tundu. We began climbing through the night, setting off at 9 p.m., aiming to reach the summit after sunrise. 'The journey back down is more dangerous than going up,' Kenton had told us at the start of our adventure. For that reason all climbers push through the night to allow themselves time to descend in daylight. I thought back to 1996 when eight people, including a guide and two expedition leaders, died in a storm on their way down from the summit. A chill ran through my body as I imagined how desperate those climbers must have been, trying to find their tents in the blizzard.

Behind me were Rob and his girlfriend Anna. Also with us was a team of British doctors who were conducting a series of groundbreaking experiments which were being filmed for a BBC documentary called *Xtreme Everest*. I figured that with so many doctors on the mountain there was not going to be a safer time to summit!

For six hours I climbed in darkness and silence. I soon caught up with Ben who was struggling with another stomach complaint. He was fumbling for some medication in his top pocket. 'Are you OK?' I shouted out. 'Yes, I'll be fine, you keep going.'

I continued ahead. The only light came from my head torch, which lit an eerie path in front of me. We were on a rocky knife-edge. To the right was a 3,000 m drop into Tibet, and to the left a 2,000 m fall into Nepal. Up ahead I could see dots of light from the torches of the doctors and other climbers. In the back of my mind I was aware that no matter how careful I was, I could not account for climbers ahead of me who could send rocks hurtling down the mountain without warning. I trembled as I thought back to the Sherpa who had been knocked to his death by falling ice, taking extra care to clip myself on to the ropes for stability.

Taking one careful step at a time, I continued climbing. As I breathed in the oxygen, the valves on my mask made a weird popping sound, which broke the muffled silence. My ankles were aching from the pressure of digging the point of my boot and crampons into the wall of ice. An icy beard was forming around my mask where my breath was starting to form icicles in the perishing cold.

Eventually Rob, Anna and I reached a ledge of rock which marked the half-way point to the summit. We were 8,500 m up. I took a sip of the water in my rucksack but it had turned to icy slush. It was still dark. Looking up, all I could see was a string of lights reaching into the sky. It was hard to tell where the light from the head torches ended and the stars in the sky began.

'My toes are so cold!' I shouted to Anna.

'Mine too!' she replied. We knew we had to do something to get them warm again and began rotating our ankles and shaking our legs to get some warm blood to our feet.

An hour of climbing later, the rising sun began to cast a warm orange shadow over the surrounding Himalayan peaks as the first light of dawn started to break. It was the most beautiful sight I have ever seen. Looking out as far as the eye could see I witnessed an orange glow around the edges of the earth. At this height, the point where the sky met the earth was thousands of miles away and was curved and radiant. I was cold and tired, but warmed by the spectacle of natural light. Looking straight down the mountain the camps below were still in darkness. It really did feel like you could touch the sky.

Exhausted, I reached the South Summit. But I still hadn't made it to the top. There was another downward climb before the final summit. At this point I started to worry, when I realised that Ben had fallen way behind the rest of our group. 'Can we call him?' I asked Rob, who had our radio link.

'Don't worry about Ben,' he said, 'he's with

Topchen the Sherpa. He'll be all right.' The radio was for use in an emergency and Rob was reluctant to waste the short battery life on unnecessary calls.

Just a few more hundred feet and the Hillary Step now stood between us and the summit. Named after Sir Edmund Hillary, who was the first person to scale it on the way to the summit with Sherpa Tenzing, it was our last challenge. And what a challenge it was. A 12 m-high rock face, covered in weathered and frozen rope. I had to clip myself onto the rope for safety, but it was difficult to tell which ropes were new and secure and which were old and worn. To be safe, I clipped onto all of them and pulled myself ever upwards. The extra effort left me gasping for breath and I turned up the flow of oxygen into my mask.

Over the step, and the rope ended. 'Not much further,' I kept telling myself as I took painfully slow steps, inching closer to my goal. I thought back to my nan's wise words: 'There's no such word as can't', and told myself I could do it if I put one foot in front of the other, one step at a time.

And there it was. The summit of Everest. The roof of the world. The pinnacle of human endurance. It was 7.30 a.m. and I had been climbing non-stop for more than ten hours. Now, just twenty steps stood between me and the summit. Each step left me gasping for breath and I was forced to stop for a few seconds to recover before taking the next one. But a huge smile began to form across my face. I took off my oxygen mask and breathed in the thin, crisp summit air. 'This is it, we've done it!' I shouted out to the wind and hugged Anna and Rob excitedly. The summit was smaller than I expected, just large enough for two or three climbers to huddle together and celebrate. A Perspex box containing a small golden Buddha statue marked the high point and the surrounding snow was littered with a jumbled collection of empty oxygen bottles, faded and frayed prayer flags and photographs of strangers: loved ones of the climbers who had been before me. I found it difficult to take everything in.

It had been a nerve-wracking experience climbing in the darkness, not knowing what lay ahead, but it was worth it. For forty minutes, bunched together with Anna and Rob, I sat on the summit and took in the spectacle, marvelling at the most extreme view in the world.

Thousands of metres below me the clouds formed a layer of whiteness, with the black harshness of the huge rugged peaks slicing through. Above me the intensity of the sky was such a deep blue, it looked almost black. Beyond the peaks, far off on the distant horizon, the blueness of the sky hugged the roundness of the earth's edge. Despite the harsh, dangerous conditions, I was overwhelmed by the feeling of purity and cleanliness of the landscape below. There is nothing on this planet that is higher at this moment, I thought. Nothing can obscure this view. Only aeroplanes and spaceships could climb higher.

It was a perfect summit day. I took out my video camera. I wanted to capture this moment for ever. But as I filmed my achievement, my voice struggled to be heard above the relentless winds which battered the summit.

Back down on the ridge, where we had just emerged, the line of other climbers snaked its way towards us. They looked like coloured dots in the distance. I hoped that Ben was one of them.

My face was swollen, my eyes were bulging from the altitude and icicles were hanging from my nose and mouth, where my breath had frozen. But I was proud. The vision I had had eighteen months ago was real. Sixty-one days had passed since I had said goodbye to my family at Heathrow Airport. As I turned once again to view the panorama, it hit me: I was standing in a place where no Welsh woman had ever stood before. The preparation and the training had paid off. I had become the first Welsh woman to reach the summit of Everest. Pulling my Welsh flag out of my bag, I posed for a photograph.

But this was not the place for celebration – that could come later. I knew that if anything were to go wrong now I was far away from help and I needed to get down safely. On the way down I passed Ben who was making good progress despite feeling very ill. We exchanged words of encouragement and I continued down the knife-edge ridge. Ben made the summit an hour later. Although separated in reaching the summit, we were united in our success.

Two days later we reached the safety of Base Camp and were greeted by our fellow climbers and Sherpas. To celebrate we opened a can of San Miguel lager. It was the best I have ever tasted! Our months of hard work and preparation had become a reality. I could not stop smiling.

Chapter Ten

INSPIRING OTHERS

On my return home to Britain, I was caught up in the post-Everest glow. Physically I was smaller than I had ever been, having lost 5 kg during the seventy-two days away in Nepal, but inside I walked tall. I thought to myself: I've done it, I've climbed Everest. How many people can actually say that? An emotional welcome was waiting for Ben and me when we arrived back at Heathrow Airport and into the arms of our families on 5 June. My mum, dad and sister were so relieved to see us. They admitted how worried they had been during the two days when we were climbing to the summit and there had been no news. But once they knew we were safe, they could be proud.

There was no time to stand around patting one another on the back. I had to race back to Cardiff with Mum, where I had been invited to a Prince's Trust gala dinner at the Wales Millennium Centre. It was almost surreal. Just days earlier I had been living on ice in a tent with no showers and hair so greasy I couldn't bear to touch it. Now I was sitting in a posh hair salon in Cardiff Bay, having my hair styled ready to meet HRH Prince Charles, founder of the Prince's Trust. Our successful expedition had raised £10,000 for his charity and it was an honour to meet him. It also made a welcome change to dress up after three months of living in padded clothes and thermal underwear. At the dinner I also met the opera star Bryn Terfel, whose deep baritone voice had soothed me and spurred me on up Everest.

Ben and I enjoyed returning to a life without the intense training routines and enjoyed cooking together, eating things that weren't available on Everest. We moved into a new flat in London and proudly displayed an enormous panorama of the summit and the south-west ridge. We relived our expedition by watching a BBC documentary which was made about the climb during which Ben admitted on camera that it was the most scary thing he had ever done.

Once I had recovered from the initial excitement and the satisfaction of achieving my dream, I had to face reality. I had no job and no real idea what I would do next. I started job hunting and soon found that being able to write 'climbed to the summit of Everest' on a job application opened doors. I was interviewed for many jobs which were way beyond my actual qualifications, just because the recruiters were curious to meet the 25-year-old Welsh girl who had the grit and guts to climb Everest. I found a fantastic job working for Make Your Mark, a campaign which encouraged and supported people to start their own business. I could relate to people who had business ideas and were looking for ways to make their ambitions real. In many ways it reflected my own experience in preparing for Everest. To make any idea a reality requires flair, commitment and determination.

Two years after the expedition, Ben and I finally agreed to end our relationship. Everest had brought us together, and neither of us could have done it without the encouragement and support of the other, but we accepted that we were not meant to be together for ever. It was an incredibly sad time to split from someone with whom I had shared so much, both the highs and the lows, but we accepted it was time to move on. I moved back to Wales where I started working for Sport Wales in Carmarthen and Ben continued working for Merrill Lynch finance company in the City of London.

Looking back on my achievement and the cold and dangerous time I spent on Everest I have learnt many personal lessons. I've developed a greater understanding of what I can achieve. I'm more able to ignore people when they say, 'You can't do that.' Actually you can with the right words of encouragement. It all goes back to those wise words of my nan: 'There's no such word as can't.' If you tell yourself you can do something, you will.

Sport and fitness remains one of the most important elements of my life. Whether it's a run around my home in Cardiff Bay after work or an entire weekend spent in the mountains, it's something I cannot be without. I love to challenge myself physically, I love the friendship of a team event, and I love being out in all weathers and seasons, appreciating beautiful natural scenery along the way. Small events such as 'Tough Guy', a gruelling muddy cross-country assault course, can give me a quick fix of adventure, but every couple of years I am looking for the next big adventure. In 2010, I ventured to New Zealand with my friend Maria Leijerstam and cycled the length of both islands, a total of 2,400 km. It was a tough cycle, but nothing in comparison with the hardships faced on Everest.

I enjoy sharing my experiences and lessons learnt on Everest with others, too. I am regularly invited to speak at charity events, or awards ceremonies, or to give talks to young people or inspire business leaders. My talks aim to inspire and to motivate. It gives me a real buzz when I receive emails from people who have listened to my talk and have been inspired to follow their dreams. I hope that through my own experiences I can be a role model for young girls to discover sport and the outdoors. I want them to know that you can be wearing a waterproof jacket and trousers one minute and reaching for your favourite high heels the next. I love living my life of extremes: covered in mud from a cross-country run, then hair styled, make-up done the next. I want young people to realise that there are adventurous opportunities on their doorsteps.

'If you really want to achieve something, it's a question of starting small, creating building blocks and putting them together in the right order,' I tell them. 'It's all very well saying "I'd like to be able to run a marathon in a year's time," but if you do nothing for the first six months, your chances are going to be pretty slim. You need to have a plan and be realistic. But more than anything you need to have a vision to see yourself achieving your goal and you should never give up, even when the going gets tough.'

But the question I am asked all the time is 'What next?' My memories of Everest and the achievement fill me with pride every single day but this question is not that easy to answer.

I recognise that I always need something to aim for. I'm lost without a goal in my life as I am not very good at sitting still and doing nothing. The challenges that really inspire and motivate me are the long journeys to remote, mostly cold, places with spectacular scenery. There is something I love about being in a tent, miles from anywhere, with the stove roaring, sharing stories with locals or team mates, knowing that you're safe in extreme conditions and self sufficient.

Overseas travel, meeting new people and different cultures broadens the mind and can develop a new outlook on everyday life. Life becomes very simple, in contrast to a busy working life at home with constant distractions. But there is also that element of risk and of pain. The achievement becomes bigger when the risk is greater and the physical challenge more demanding.

It's the feeling of achievement that I crave. The feeling you get when you sit on the sofa with a cup of tea after a twenty-mile run and say, 'I did it'. It doesn't have to be Everest. I know that a lack of time and money can act as barriers to achieving our dreams, but I've learnt that if you want to do something enough you'll find a way to overcome them. With passion, planning and self-belief you can achieve more than you ever thought possible.

Remember your next adventure could be just around the corner.

Quick Reads 📖

Fall in love with reading

Grand Slam Man
Dan Lydiate

Accent Press

When Wales beat France to clinch the 2012 Six Nations Championship Grand Slam – one player stood out from the rest of the field.

A powerful presence on the pitch, Dan Lydiate, the 6ft 4in fearless farmer's son truly deserved the title Player of the Tournament.

In *Grand Slam Man*, the heroic Welsh flanker reflects on his comeback from a broken neck in 2008 to become the hero of Wales's 2012 Grand Slam success. He also reveals his thoughts on the Australia tour, his love of tackling, his life on the farm and his British Lions dream.

About the Author

Tori James grew up on her family farm in Pembrokeshire. She first entered the record books as a member of the first ever all-female team to complete The Polar Challenge, a 360 mile race to the Magnetic North Pole. Her climb to the summit of Everest in 2007 was featured in the BBC documentary *On Top of the World*.

Tori works as a community liaison leader and is also a motivational speaker.